Learning From The Lizard

Bible Animal Object Lessons

Samuel J. Hahn

Illustrations by
Scott Patton

CSS Publishing Company, Inc., Lima, Ohio

LEARNING FROM THE LIZARD

Copyright © 2000 by
CSS Publishing Company, Inc.
Lima, Ohio

The original purchaser may photocopy material in this publication for use as it was intended (i.e., worship material for worship use; educational material for classroom use; dramatic material for staging or production). No additional permission is required from the publisher for such copying by the original purchaser only. Inquiries should be addressed to: Permissions, CSS Publishing Company, Inc., P.O. Box 4503, Lima, Ohio 45802-4503.

Scripture quotations identified (NRSV) are from the *New Revised Standard Version of the Bible*, copyright 1989 by the Division of Christian Education of the National Council of the Churches of Christ in the USA. Used by permission.

Scripture quotations identified (TEV) are from the Good News Bible, in Today's English Version. Copyright © American Bible Society 1966, 1971, 1976. Used by permission.

Scripture quotations identified (KJV) are from the *King James Version of the Bible*, in the public domain.

Scripture quotations marked (TLB) are taken from *The Living Bibl*e © 1971. Used by permission of Tyndale House Publishers, Inc., Wheaton, IL 60189. All rights reserved.

Scripture quotations marked (RSV) are taken from the *Revised Standard Version of the Bible*, copyrighted 1946, 1952 ©, 1971, 1973, by the Division of Christian Education of the National Council of the Churches of Christ in the USA. Used by permission.

ISBN 0-7880-1593-1   PRINTED IN U.S.A.

Author's Dedication

I would like to dedicate this book to my children, Eunice, Jonathan, and Deborah; my grandchildren, Benjaman, Mathew, and Adam; my charming wife Juanita; and in memory of my parents, Henry and Carrie Hahn.

Each one of these has touched and blessed my life in a significant way!

Above all, this is dedicated to God, to his glory and his purpose!

— *Samuel J. Hahn*

Artist's Dedication

I would like to dedicate the art in this book to my parents, Jim and Annice Patton, who have always encouraged me in my artistic pursuits, and to my Lord, the source of my gift.

— *Scott Patton*

Table Of Contents

Preface	7
Foreword	9
Ant: The Wise Worker	11
Bear: A Diligent Provider For Family	13
Camel: Prepared for Storms	17
Cattle Or Oxen: The Ox Knows Its Owner	19
Coney: Life Can Be Fragile	22
Crow Or Raven: A Purpose In Common Things	25
Deer: A Longing For God	27
Donkey: Jesus Rides In Triumph	31
Dove: Symbol Of The Holy Spirit	33
Eagle: He Gives Power	37
Eagle: Renewing Youthfulness	39
Fox: Amazing Ability To Adapt	43
Goat: Basic Provider For Basic Needs	45
Honey Bee: A Willing Worker	49
Lion: Boldness	51

Lizard: Inconspicuous, Yet Clever	54
Locust: A Warning From God	56
Ostrich: Strength For Sensational Speed	59
Owl: Wisdom Is A Virtue	63
Peacock: Beauty — A Gift From God	67
Pelican: Sacrificial Care For Others	69
Quail: God's Abundant Provision	73
Rooster Or Chicken: A Call To Watchfulness	75
Sheep: Follow The Leader	79
Sparrow: I Know He Cares For Me	81

Preface

The Bible is filled with a variety of fascinating and intriguing references to birds, animals, and insects. As we look at the wonders of God's Creation, there are strengthening lessons that we can learn.

The writer of the Proverbs gave us these words of wisdom:

> *Four things on earth are small,*
>   *yet they are exceedingly wise:*
> *the ants are a people without strength,*
>   *yet they provide their food in the summer;*
> *the badgers are a people without power,*
>   *yet they make their homes in the rocks;*
> *the locusts have not a king*
>   *yet all of them march in rank;*
> *the lizard or the spider can be grasped in the hand,*
>   *yet it is found in kings' palaces.*
>   — Proverbs 30:24-28 NRSV

We will consider the ways of the ant and be wise, and learn from him some renewing spiritual truths! We will "mount up with wings like eagles" and learn a lesson there, too. We may even follow that spider into the king's palace.

All statements of science and nature have been carefully researched and are scientifically accurate. Occasionally additional Bible references are given which provide further information.

We recommend the use of this booklet as a gift, a daily devotional guide, children's sermon illustrations, or simply inspirational, uplifting reading.

Scott Patton, a superb nature artist from Perry, Iowa, has done the art work. He researched the animals and completed the detailed drawings to be true to the animals living in the area of Palestine.

Foreword

Recently a friend called asking for my help with her daughter, a student at the University of Iowa, telling of the death of a favorite pet. She was grieving the loss of the pet, especially after someone had told her that according to the Bible, animals never go to heaven. Just prior to that time in a morning devotional I had read Psalm 36 which includes:

> *Your righteousness is like the mighty mountains,*
> *your judgments are like the great deep;*
> *you save humans and animals alike, O Lord.*
> *How precious is your steadfast love, O God!*
> *All people may take refuge in the shadow of your wings.*
> — Psalm 36:6-7 NRSV

And as it is translated in TEV:

> *Your righteousness is towering like the mountains;*
> *Your justice is like the depths of the sea.*
> *People and animals are in your care.*
> *How precious, O God, is your constant love!*
> *We find protection under the shadow of your wings.*

I'm not sure of the total meaning of "... you save humans and animals alike ... are under your care ..." But it makes a good case for the quality of life God provides, even for animals. And I guess it could be that since life here is so wondrously enhanced with animal life, that in heaven, "paradise," there may be the song of birds and the opportunity to cuddle a puppy or a kitty.

Interesting, isn't it, that in verse seven above, the biblical writer uses another animal symbol, comparing God's care to the protective wings of a mother bird.

Whatever life situation you may be facing, I believe the pages of this book can be enriching, strengthening, and supportive.

I have not tried to exhaust the implications and lessons from the animals included. Entire books could be and have been written about each animal. In this book "animal" is used in a general sense, including mammals, birds, reptiles, and insects.

We live at a time of growing interest in wildlife. Fortunately some animals, including the majestic bald eagle, have been brought back from the brink of extinction. Readers will be challenged to see how they fit into God's plan of providing care for all animals and preserving wildlife for all generations to come. We can find hope in the awareness that naturalists in Palestine today are also deeply involved in preserving nature. The Society for the Protection of Nature in Israel has become a key for the survival of wildlife.

Ant

The Wise Worker

Go to the ant you lazybones; consider its ways, and be wise. Without having any chief or officer it prepares its food in summer, and gathers its sustenance in harvest (Proverbs 6:6-8 NRSV).

The writer of Proverbs must have been a real student of ant behavior. Ants are wise! Ant colonies might be compared to cities. Hundreds, sometimes thousands, of ants live in one nest. They have a designed division of labor, carefully organized. Some workers bring food to the colony; some feed and care for the young. Others keep the colony clean or store food away. Some guard against intruders.

Some species of ants have amazing food gathering and storage procedures. Some ants keep aphids or leaf hoppers for honeydew just as a farmer keeps cows. The "cows" are herded to the proper plants, then the ants "milk" the honeydew by stroking the insects with their antennae. The honeydew is a liquid secretion of the aphid. Leafcutter ants raise their own edible mushrooms that grow on leaves they carry into their nest. Harvester ants gather seeds inside their nests for a future food supply. Ants are strong enough to carry loads many times heavier than themselves.

Lessons From The Ant

Work hard! The work ethic is all right as long as we take time for home, family, and God. Work hard toward spiritual growth!

Respect others! In their division of labor some ants are assigned to lowly tasks. In God's sight all honest labor is important.

Care for the young! Throughout the world there are times when children are neglected. Their demands should not rule our lives, but taking priority time for them and leading exemplary lives for them are basic.

Save for the future! Good stewardship involves the awareness that God is owner of all, and that he calls us to be wise caretakers of all he has given us.

Prayer

Lord of life and nature, thank you for lessons from a lowly ant. Speak to us in terms of diligence and dedication. Thank you for the challenge of work and the opportunity most of us have to work. Where there are those who are jobless, we pray that the economy and educational opportunities will be such that work will be available. We pray in the name of The Master Workman of the Race, even our Lord Jesus. Amen.

Bear

A Diligent Provider For Family

Better to meet a she-bear robbed of its cubs than to confront a fool immersed in folly (Proverbs 17:12 NRSV).

The bear is mentioned thirteen times in the Old Testament and once in the New. Although it is mainly dependent on plant fruits or berries, it also is carnivorous and will eat lambs or other small animals. When winter approaches and food is not available, a bear depends on hibernation.

The bear referred to in the Bible is most likely the brown bear, which can attain a size of six feet tall and weigh as much as 500 pounds. It is much smaller than a polar or grizzly bear.

At birth the baby bear weighs only one-half pound, and is very dependent on its mother. The mother rightfully shows much fury in protecting her young. A most dangerous animal to encounter would be the she bear with cubs, or even more dangerous, robbed of her cubs. Several Bible passages refer to this. "You know that your father David and his men are hard fighters and that they are as fierce as a mother bear robbed of her cubs" (2 Samuel 17:8 TEV). See also Hosea 13:8.

A wicked ruler is compared to a "roaring lion or a raging bear" (Proverbs 28:15) and one of the signs of the Peaceable Kingdom is: "Cows and bears will eat together and their calves and cubs will lie down in peace" (Isaiah 11:7 TEV).

Another colorful proverbial expression comes from the Prophet Amos: "How terrible it will be for you who long for the day of the Lord ... For it will be a day of darkness and not light. It will be like a man who runs from a lion and meets a bear" (Amos 5:18 TEV). This was given as a part of a call to repentance, without which the Day of the Lord would come upon them as disaster and judgment.

The Peaceable Kingdom is further described:

> *On Zion, God's sacred hill,*
> *there will be nothing*
> *harmful or evil.*
> *The land will be as full of*
> *knowledge of the Lord*
> *as the seas are full of water*
> — Isaiah 11:9 TEV

Lessons From The Bear

Be diligent in providing for your children. Be as a guardian for them, a supportive safe haven, perhaps even a shelter in time of storm.

Prayer

Gracious and loving God, as a part of creation you have made animals that can be destructive. Teach us to respect the forces of nature we cannot control. Help us to be a part of the "Peaceable Kingdom," where swords will be turned into plowshares, and we will learn war no more. In Jesus' name may we even be able to love our enemies, and pray for those who despitefully use us. In the name of the Prince of Peace. Amen.

Camel

Prepared For Storms

"It is easier for a camel to go through the eye of the needle than for someone who is rich to enter the kingdom of God ... For mortals it is impossible, but not for God; for God all things are possible" (Mark 10:25, 27 NRSV).

No animal is better prepared for the devastating storms of the desert than the camel. Our scripture verse suggests the storm of difficulty some have in being true disciples, but with God all things are possible.

Scientists tell us that the camel has been man's servant for longer than any other creature. Not only is it capable of providing transportation in the nearly impossible desert terrain, but it also provides milk, cheese, hair for blankets and tents, and even meat. Mark 1:6 speaks of John the Baptist as clothed with camel's hair. In transportation of goods, the camel can carry as much as 1,000 pounds.

God the Creator did a masterful job in preparing the camel for the desert. The eyes are protected by over-hanging lids and long lashes which shield it from the intense sun. The nostrils can be closed tight against the driving sand of the storms. The camel's upper lip can reach out for shrubs, and its very strong teeth can chew almost anything. If no other food is around it can eat leather, blankets, bones, or whole fish. It will even drink salty water. Nothing seems to give it indigestion. An added feature, its large two-toed feet are especially cushioned for walking on the sand.

We have assumed that the Wise Men bringing their gifts to Jesus traveled by camel, but the Bible doesn't state that. Camels might indicate great wealth; Job after his suffering was blessed with 6,000 camels.

Lessons From The Camel

Meet the storms on your knees. The camel is not known for its obedience or intelligence, except when it faces a storm. When the wind begins to blow strong enough to blow sand, the camel drops to its knees, closes its nostrils, stretches out its neck, and remains motionless until the storm has passed, thus protecting itself and its rider.

Carry your burdens patiently. Although stubborn, once loaded and started the camel will patiently carry its load great distances. Often our burdens seem more than we can bear. With God's help the load can be mastered, perhaps even turned into a cross-crown of glory (Mark 8:34-37).

Prayer

Dear Lord, we have seen how the camel is one of your helpful servants providing service and produce in many ways. May we willingly take up the cross, carry our burdens, and be prepared spiritually for any storms of trouble that may come our way. We pray in the name of him who said: "My yoke is easy and my burden is light." Amen.

Other Scriptures About The Camel
    Isaiah 60:6
    Jeremiah 2:23
    Exodus 9:3

Cattle Or Oxen

The Ox Knows Its Owner

For every wild animal of the forest is mine, the cattle on a thousand hills. I know all the birds of the air, and all that moves in the field is mine (Psalm 50:10-11 NRSV).

Cattle or oxen and words referring to them are used 450 times in the Bible. Some of these terms are "bull," "bullock," "cow," "heifer," and "kine," used in the Bible as the plural of cow. The ox is usually referred to as a beast of burden, an adult castrated male. But at times the Bible refers to either bulls, male, or cows, female, as being used to work the land or to pull carts. In fact, the Hebrew word for ox, *baqar*, may refer to either gender. For some types of work cows were favored over bulls. The instructions given in 1 Samuel 6 for moving the Ark of the Covenant were that two "kine" or cows should be used, being considered more gentle for the sacred task.

Since cattle were so essential to everyday living in Bible times, the Mosaic laws made special provision for their Sabbath rest (Exodus 23:12) and special provision if straying (Deuteronomy 22:1; Exodus 23:4). Even a fallen ox was to be helped to its feet: "You shall not see your neighbor's donkey or ox fallen on the road and ignore it; you shall help to lift it up" (Deuteronomy 22:4 NRSV).

Cattle, a most prized possession, were the most valuable of sacrifices. Some of the symbolic instruction is given in Exodus 29:10-12: "You shall bring the bull in front of the tent meeting. Aaron and his sons shall lay their hands on the head of the bull, and you shall slaughter the bull before the Lord ... and you shall take some of the blood of the bull and put it on the horns of the altar" (NRSV). (See also 1 Kings 8:63 and 2 Chronicles 5:6.)

Cattle were a basic source of food. They were very important for the highest quality meat. The quality was enhanced if the animal was kept stalled for fattening. When the prodigal son returned, the "fatted calf" was prepared for the feast. (See also Proverbs

15:17.) Milk and cheese were very important parts of the diet. Because of the hot climate butter was not often used. Curds, similar to cottage cheese, were a favorite food. Yes, multipurpose cattle were so important that their product of milk was used to describe the promised land as "a land flowing with milk and honey!" (Exodus 3:8).

Lessons From The Ox

The prophet Isaiah brings to mind a basic truth that any farmer knows, but one Israel had failed to learn. "The ox knows its owner, and the donkey its master's crib; but Israel does not know, my people do not understand." Cattle when cared for are faithful workers, faithful and generous in supplying milk, and they know and follow their keeper's guidance. As Christians can we be less faithful or appreciative?

Prayer

Gracious God, you are so generous in providing for the needs of humanity. Thank you for the ample supply of food, meat, milk, cheese, and other food products that come from cattle to enrich our lives. Also you bless us with leather for shoes and garments that we so easily take for granted. We pray that you will guide us to use wisely the gift of animal life you have given to our care. We include in our prayers such work as Heifer Project that makes cattle available to those places in the world that need so much an added milk and food supply. Out of our abundance may we continually reach out to share with others. In Jesus' name. Amen.

Coney

Life Can Be Fragile

The conies are but a feeble folk, yet they make their houses among the rocks (Proverbs 30:26 KJV).

The coney, also known as the rock hyrax or the rock badger, weighs about seven pounds. It is about the same shape as a prairie dog with a thick gray brown body and short sturdy legs. Its toes are connected with folds of skin and the soles of its feet are equipped with pads kept moist by special glands. These result in natural "suction cups" that enable the coney to climb the steepest and most slippery rock surfaces.

The conies live together in colonies, similar to prairie dogs, and also post guards that with a sharp whistle alarm, sends the colony to immediate shelter. Not well equipped to dig in soil, their colonies are in rocky areas or on cliffs. Their diet consists of leaves, roots, bulbs, and other plant food. They have a long gestation period of seven months.

"The high hills are a refuge for the wild goats and the rocks for the conies" (Psalm 104:18 KJV). The writer of Proverbs lists the coney among the four things which are little upon the earth and yet exceedingly wise (Proverbs 30:26). Yes, "cliff badgers are delicate little animals who protect themselves by living among the rocks" (Proverbs 30:26 TLB).

Lessons From The Coney

Care for others. The coney lives in a community with each one helping others and warning each other of danger. We certainly could be more supportive of each other.

Accept limitations. Though often living on high cliffs the coney cannot fly. In fact, hawks and eagles are a serious threat to them. They can accept their limitations and warn each other, finding safety if threatened. Few of us are strong and powerful, so living with limitations is for us also a mark of wisdom.

Prayer

Dear Lord, you are our rock and our protection. In times of trouble we can call upon you and know your protective power and strength. Be with those who consider themselves weak or feeble. Like the wise coney may we care for each other. Lift us into your love in Jesus' name. Amen.

Crow Or Raven

A Purpose In Common Things

"Consider the ravens: they neither sow nor reap, they have neither storehouse nor barn, and yet God feeds them. Of how much more value are you than the birds!" (Luke 12:24 NRSV).

The very first bird mentioned in the Bible is the raven. At the time of the Flood, Genesis 8:6-7 puts it this way: "At the end of forty days Noah opened the window of the ark that he had made and sent out the raven; and it went to and fro until the waters were dried up from the earth" (Genesis 8:6-7 NRSV). The raven with tremendous endurance will roam far from its home in search of food. Perhaps we can assume that the raven, some place far from the ark, did find food and had no reason to return. The raven or crow was thought to be able to smell land at a great distance and was often taken on early voyages of exploration for that purpose.

The crow family includes jays, ravens, magpies, rooks, jackdaws, and fish crows. The word "raven" is most often used in the Bible. There are ten references to raven in the Old Testament. The Hebrew word is *oreb* and literally means "the black one." The one reference in the New Testament is given above.

Mosaic law did not allow the raven to be used as food. But in 1 King 17:4-6 the ravens brought food to Elijah at the beginning of the drought that ravaged Israel. They are mentioned as indications of God's protective love (Job 38:41, Psalm 147:9 and Luke 12:24). The Psalm passage says: "He gives to the animals their food, and to the young ravens when they cry." The black luster of the raven's beautiful feathers is brought to mind in the Song of Solomon 5:11 where the beloved is described: "His locks are wavy, black as a raven."

Crows or ravens are very intelligent birds. They can easily be tamed as pets and can imitate sounds; sometimes they are even taught to speak as well as parrots do. Crows can be destructive to other smaller birds and crops, but are helpful insect eaters. To their credit, scientists have estimated that crows eat nineteen bushels of insects in a single season on the average farm.

Lessons From The Crow

The crow is sometimes considered to be an ugly, dirty, or cruel bird, but even so, we have noted how God cares for and uses them. The common things of life do have a real purpose in God's creative and unique plan.

Prayer

Gracious Lord, you have told us to "consider the ravens" because you care for them. Thank you for reminding us that we don't have to worry about what we will eat or wear. Instead may we seek first your Kingdom, and may we reach out to provide help and care for those less fortunate than we, who do not have sufficient food, clothing, or housing. May we find true areas of service among the least and lost of the world. We pray in the name of Jesus who came to serve all. Yes, Lord! Amen.

Deer

A Longing For God

As a deer longs for a stream of cool water, so I long for you, O God. I thirst for you, the living God (Psalm 42:1-2 TEV).

Although the word "deer" does not occur in the King James Version of the Bible, there are references to "hart" (eleven times), "hind" (ten times), and "fallow deer" (two times). Roebuck and roe most likely refer to the gazelle, which is discussed later.

At the present time deer are nearly extinct in the Palestine area. In biblical times there is evidence of three types of deer, the red deer, the fallow deer, and the roe deer. Deer meat was considered a great delicacy and was plentiful in King Solomon's sophisticated court kitchen (1 Kings 4:23).

The insightful Hebrew authors showed a remarkable ability to observe the deer's characteristics and habits. They stressed the deer's beauty and stately carriage which turned their thoughts to noble heroes. Habakkuk says: "The Sovereign Lord gives me strength. He makes me sure-footed as a deer and keeps me safe on the mountains" (Habakkuk 3:19 TEV). Another symbolic statement from the Song of Solomon speaks of the bridegroom as a "... young stag upon rugged mountains" (Song of Solomon 2:17).

The deer's leaping ability and sure-footedness was clearly observed and provides the setting for a famous passage in Isaiah in which he speaks of the joy of the redeemed: "The lame man will leap up like a deer, and those who could not speak will shout and sing!" (Isaiah 35:6 TLB).

Having observed the dark, gentle eyes and graceful limbs of the roe deer, the writer of Proverbs compares this to the charm of a woman: "So be happy with your wife and find your joy with the girl you married — pretty and graceful as a deer. Let her charms keep you happy; let her surround you with her love" (Proverbs 5:18-19 TEV).

The most familiar passage about deer is that given for the opening, Psalm 42:1-2. With the picture of a thirsty deer the writer has successfully dramatized the intense thirst for spiritual refreshment. In a country where droughts are prevalent during the hot summer this truth is especially meaningful.

Lessons From The Deer
Hunger and thirst for righteousness. Food and water provide physical satisfaction, but only the Living Water from our Lord can provide the inner satisfaction whereby we will never thirst again.

Prayer
Creator God, the scriptures speak in colorful pictures of the gracefulness and swiftness of the deer. May we be swift to do your will and graceful in our service of others. Forgive us for so often depending on our strength alone. May our longing for you find full satisfaction in your love for us through Jesus our Lord. Yes, Lord. Amen!

Donkey

Jesus Rides In Triumph

He told them, "Go into the village ahead of you, and as you enter it you will find tied there a colt that has never been ridden. Untie it and bring it here. If anyone asks, 'Why are you untying it?' just say this, 'The Lord needs it' " (Luke 19:30-31 NRSV).

Older versions use the term "ass" for donkey or colt. The "donkey" of the Bible is much different than donkeys known in the United States.

An Encyclopedia of Bible Animals points out: "Our donkeys are usually quite small, and are obstinate and rather mean animals that (not without reason) are accused of being stupid. But in warmer climates this animal develops into a large, pretty and stately animal ... In fact the Hebrew name for the ass, *chamor,* literally means 'tawny'; Deborah challenges those 'who ride on tawny asses' to join in the praise of God for the victory that has been won (Judges 5:10). It is no accident then that biblical authors never mention the stubbornness, the meanness, or the laziness that we associate with the 'donkey.' These are traits that a Near Easterner would never see in this animal."[1]

The donkey is not as swift as a horse, but in mountainous terrain it is much more sure-footed and able to travel greater distances without food and water. In Bible times the donkey was used for riding, as a pack animal, and even in war. For these purposes the female was preferred because of greater stamina and because they were less prone to distractions.

Unless the family was wealthy enough to have more than one animal, the wife would ride and the husband walked alongside. As Exodus 4:20 says: "So Moses took his wife and his sons, put them on a donkey and set out with them for Egypt, carrying the walking stick that God had told him to take" (RSV).

A man riding on a donkey became a symbol of the Prince of Peace. (See Zachariah 9:9.) So Jesus, in fulfillment, rides into Jerusalem leaving no doubt as to the nature of his Kingdom.

Throughout the Bible the donkey is spoken of as very valuable and a true measure of wealth. The wealthy Job had 500 female donkeys before disaster struck him; then when his property, health, and family were restored he had 1,000.

Lessons From The Donkey

We are called to be peace makers. Instead of a war horse as used by the Romans, Jesus as the Prince of Peace entered Jerusalem on Palm Sunday on a donkey as a humble servant; yet he was truly King of kings.

Prayer

Gracious Prince of Peace, we pray for peace — peace in our hearts and peace throughout the whole world. "Let there be peace on earth, and let it begin with me." May your peace come to troubled hearts. May peace come to those places in the world where war, violence, and abuse are present. Thank you for the gift of peace. In Jesus' name. Amen.

---

1. Peter France, *An Encyclopedia of Bible Animals* (Croom-Helm, 1986). Used by permission of Routledge Publishing, London.

Dove

Symbol Of The Holy Spirit

I wish I had wings like a dove. I would fly away and find rest (Psalm 55:6 TEV).

Biblical writers for the most part were keen observers of nature and wild life. One bird written about with such skill is the dove.

In Israel there is an abundance of many species of doves, pigeons, and turtle doves, including the rock dove. Jeremiah 48:28 refers to the rock dove: "You people who live in Moab, leave your towns! Go and live on the cliffs! Be like the dove that makes its nest in the sides of a ravine" (TEV). The domestic pigeon seen in such abundance today is a descendent of the rock dove.

Genesis 8:8 and following tells how Noah sent out a dove as the water was receding after the flood. First it returned with nothing because the flood covered all. Then when released later it returned with a fresh olive leaf, evidence that the flood was receding.

The references to the "love bird" characteristics of the dove provide some of the most picturesque and romantic statements of the Bible. One of these is found in the Song of Solomon 2:13b-14: "Come then, my love; my darling, come with me. You are like a dove that hides in the crevice of a rock. Let me see your lovely face and hear your enchanting voice" (TEV). Song of Solomon 1:15 and 5:12 speak of lovers' eyes "like doves." According to tradition, doves mate for life and are so chaste that if one loses its mate it does not seek another.

Currently in art forms the dove is seen most frequently in churches as a symbol of the Holy Spirit. One of the favorite stained glass art works shows the Holy Spirit in the form of a dove descending on Jesus at the time of his baptism by John. "I saw the Spirit descend like a dove ..." (John 1:32). Above many baptismal fonts is the dove representing the same passage.

Doves were also an important part of the sacrificial system for the worship at the Temple. The lamb was the most basic animal for

a sacrifice but doves could be substituted: "If the woman cannot afford a lamb, she shall bring two doves ... one for a burnt offering and the other for a sin offering, and the priest shall perform the ritual ..." (Leviticus 12:8 TEV). Luke 2:24 tells of this being done when Jesus was presented in the Temple. "So they took the child to Jerusalem to present him to the Lord ... They also went to offer a sacrifice of a pair of doves as required by the Law of the Lord" (Luke 2:22-24 TEV).

Birds of the dove family must depend on God in a special way because they are among the world's worst nest builders. It is amazing that the little ones survive! The nest is simply and clumsily made of coarse twigs and grass. The female usually lays two white eggs. Both male and female take turns sitting on the eggs. At least two broods are raised. If weather permits they will nest the year round and raise as many as eleven broods.

Doves and pigeons have a unique style of walking that some have called a "stutter step," something like: head ahead, step, stop; head ahead, step, stop. The reason for this is that except in flight the dove cannot focus its eyes unless it stops for a fraction of a second. Doves are also unique among birds in that they can provide nourishment to their young in the form of "pigeon milk," a substance secreted by the crop.

Lessons From The Dove

Stop to focus. We tend to travel so fast in life that things are out of focus. Stopping, taking time for God, having a time to wait upon God, can help to bring life into proper focus.

Receive the Holy Spirit. The Spirit-filled life is not a radical way of life, but the way of service strengthened and guided by the presence of the Holy Spirit. It should be as gentle and beautiful as a pure white dove!

Prayer

Spirit of the Living God, you revealed yourself in the form of a dove at the time Jesus was baptized. We truly pray, "Spirit of the Living God, fall afresh on me. Melt me, mold me, fill me, use me. Spirit of the Living God, fall afresh on me." This is our prayer. Yes, Lord! Amen!

Eagle

He Gives Power

Have you not known? Have you not heard? The Lord is the everlasting God, the Creator of the ends of the earth. He does not faint or grow weary; his understanding is unsearchable. He gives power to the faint, and strengthens the powerless. Even youths will faint and be weary, and the young will fall exhausted; but those who wait for the Lord shall renew their strength. They shall mount up with wings like eagles, they shall run and not be weary, they shall walk and not faint (Isaiah 40:28-31 NRSV).

Worldwide in nearly every country and tradition, the eagle is considered a symbol of power and strength. Several of the biblical writers were well aware of this.

The word "eagle" is used 34 times in the Bible. The most famous biblical quotation is the scripture used above. If only we could mount up with wings like eagles! Or maybe we can if we believe the truth of Isaiah 40:28-31.

As we face the storms of life, are we more like a chicken or an eagle? An eagle, unless it must stay with its young or the eggs in a nest, will ride above the storm. Sensing an approaching storm it will spread its wings and rise on the thermals and vanguard winds circling ever higher and higher until at several thousand feet it is above the storm. At the same time, chickens confined to the ground may be soaked and blown around resulting in a serious sickness.

There are eight kinds of eagles known in Palestine and Israel. Most notable is the golden eagle, a giant bird with a wingspan of seven or eight feet. It is interesting that the female is more than ten percent larger than the male. With their incredible vision, about four times sharper than human vision, they can spot a rabbit from a distance of one mile or spot another eagle soaring from a distance of fifteen to thirty miles!

Lessons From The Eagle

Look to God for that renewal of strength that he provides. Take time to wait upon the Lord, especially during those times of stress, anxiety, or need.

Prayer

All-powerful and all-loving God, as we turn our eyes upon Jesus give us the clarity of vision to see your will and the strength to follow it. May we truly mount up with wings like eagles, knowing your indwelling power and strength. Yes, Lord! Amen!

Eagle

Renewing Youthfulness

I bore you on eagles' wings and brought you to myself (Exodus 19:4 RSV).

Bless the Lord, O my soul ... who satisfies you with good as long as you live so that your youth is renewed like the eagle's (Psalm 103:2, 5 RSV).

Under normal conditions eagles enjoy a very long life, often 25 years in the wild, and up to fifty years in captivity. No doubt the psalm writer quoted above saw the same pair of eagles return year after year to their nest. Eagles that never appeared to age, but continued to be vigorous and high flyers, were a part of the natural habitat.

Eagles generally mate for life and, as all wise parents should, they share in the task of raising their young. They take turns sitting on the nest for 34 or 35 days until the eaglets hatch. Then they continue to share in feeding the young.

Each year before the eggs are laid the pair of eagles add to the same nest which may become six feet deep and seven feet across — as large as a small room in a house. The nest is built high in a large tree or on high rocks in a mountainous area.

Deuteronomy 32:11 says: "As an eagle stirs up its nest ..." So it is very true that the parent eagles must coax and maybe even coerce the reluctant young to leave the nest. This happens when the fledglings are about twelve weeks old.

The passage from Exodus 19:4 gives an incredible promise from God, "I bore you on eagles' wings!" It would certainly be rare, but no doubt it has happened, that when the fledgling was jumping up from the nest to test its wings, it came down atop the nearby parent. The parent then taking flight could actually launch the young eaglet on its first flight. That may be what the biblical writer had seen.

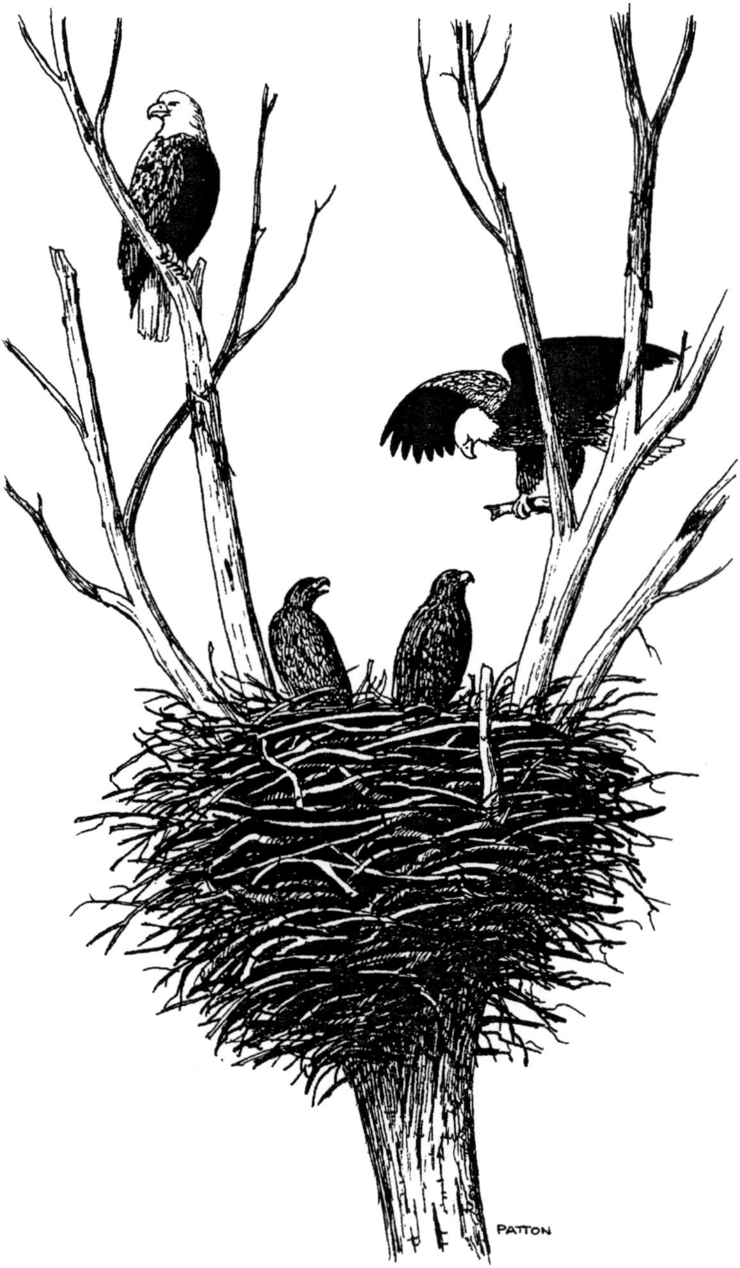
PATTON

We have all been blessed by the "Footprints in the Sand" story telling of Jesus carrying us through the most devastating times of life. (See Isaiah 63:9.) With the eagles in mind, I would like to suggest that he even carries us on his wings in those darkest hours!

Lessons From The Eagle

Make a leap of faith. God may guide us, even push us out of our safe comfortable places into areas where we can grow and serve him more completely. Flying is a risky business, but we can be lifted out of stagnation to joyful areas of exciting and dynamic service!

Prayer

Loving and lifting Lord, truly your love has lifted us. More than the wonderful awareness, that you hold us in the palm of your hands, may we truly believe that because of your love and strength, we can mount up with wings as eagles! Lift us above doubt and fear and despair into heights of service with you. In Jesus' name we believe. Yes, and Amen!

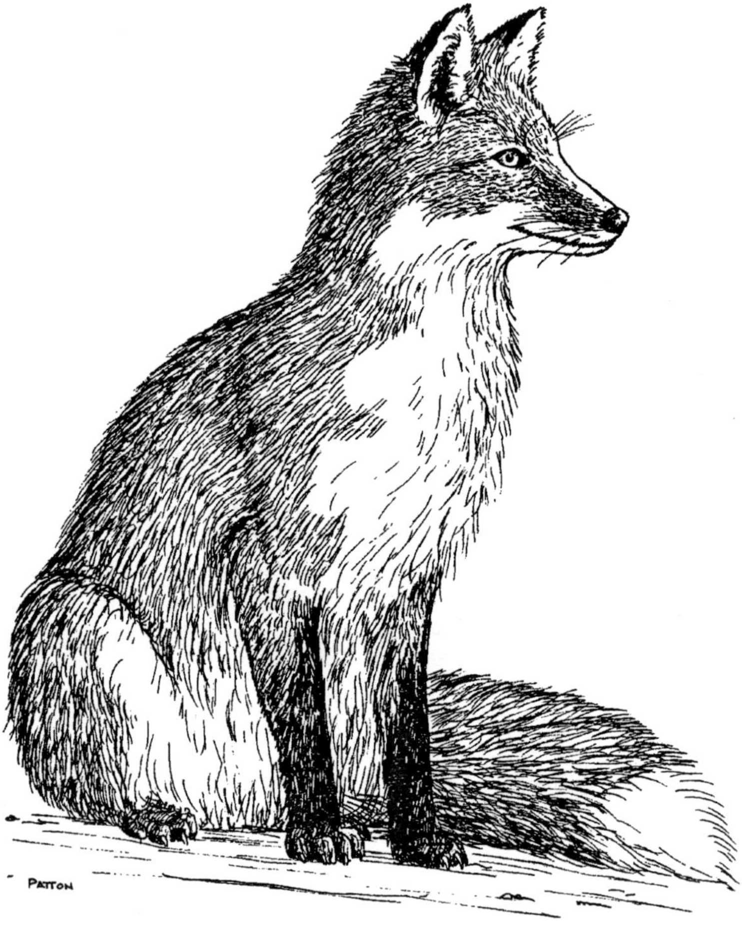
PATTON

Fox

Amazing Ability To Adapt

As they were going along the road, someone said to him, "I will follow you wherever you go." And Jesus said to him, "Foxes have holes, and birds of the air have nests; but the Son of Man has nowhere to lay his head" (Luke 9:57-58 NRSV).

With very good reason the dictionary includes these words to define a fox: "noted for craftiness ... a sly cunning fellow." Few animals show more wit or wisdom when it comes to hunting and survival. Despite being hunted, trapped, and poisoned, the fox continues in abundance as a real survivor. They have even adapted to survival within large cities.

Fox hunters can attest to the craftiness of the fox. In order to fool the hounds and to make tracking impossible, they run in stream beds or on the frozen river ice. Using unusual skill, they have been known to tread on thin ice deliberately, which supports them but not the hounds in pursuit. In England they may run away by staying on top of a stone wall. And on occasion in a formal fox hunt with hounds and horses, they have been known suddenly to race directly into the approaching pack, the hounds turning around in pursuit running into the horses and causing mass confusion!

The verses given from Luke 9:57-58 are significant reminders that he who was in the beginning with God at the time of creation provided for others and for nature, but during his earthly ministry had no home of his own!

Another passage brings to mind the keen hearing of a fox:

> *At that very hour some Pharisees came and said to him, "Get away from here, for Herod wants to kill you." He said to them, "Go and tell that fox for me, 'Listen, I am casting out demons and performing cures today and tomorrow, and on the third day I will finish my work.'"*
> — Luke 13:32 NRSV

A fox has a keen sense of hearing, and in the case of Herod, he was hearing too much, fearing that he might lose some power and popularity to Jesus. A fox, in fact, is so sensitive in hearing that what a man can hear at 175 yards a fox can easily hear at a mile.

The fox is a very beautiful animal whose pelts are highly prized. Some red foxes have an interesting "cross" marking on their backs. A dark brown stripe of hair runs the length of the back and is crossed by another dark stripe across the shoulder. In legend this has been linked to the story of Sampson in Judges 15:4-5 where foxes are caught and used to set fire to the enemy's grain fields, resulting, of course, in the foxes being scorched.

The Song of Solomon (2:15) talks about the little foxes that spoil the vineyard. The diet of foxes does consist of mice and ground squirrels, insects, fruit, and other similar food. Though occasionally they catch poultry, they prove their worth by the millions of mice and other ground rodents they catch each year.

Yes, the fox is one of God's cunning creatures!

Lessons From The Fox

Unfortunately, some types of wildlife are endangered or even completely extinct because civilization has taken their habitat. Foxes with their adaptability can make changes and adjust. In the changes we constantly face God can give us the wisdom to make the changes that are in keeping with his will, changes that enable us to survive the testing times.

Prayer

Lord God, you have reminded us to be "wise as serpents and as harmless as doves." May we be crafty and wise when we must be, in our service of you. May we see your purpose in "all things bright and beautiful, in all creatures great and small." Thank you that our Lord Jesus, though homeless during most of his ministry, provides for us now, and in his grace provides a heavenly home. Praise be to you our God! Amen!

Goat

Basic Provider For Basic Needs

The lambs will provide your clothing, and the goats the price of a field; there will be enough goats' milk for your food, for the food of your household and nourishment for your servant girls (Proverbs 27:26-27 NRSV).

The goat entered significantly into every part of Hebrew life. The goat was acceptable for a sacrifice, provided meat, milk, cheese, goat hair for spinning, and skins for shelter or carrying of liquids.

There are 124 references in the Bible to the domestic goat and there is biblical evidence of how highly valued goats were. The wealth of Nabal depended in part on his goat herd. "He was a very rich man, the owner of 3,000 sheep and 1,000 goats (1 Samuel 25:2). Jehoshaphat's wealth also included 7,700 goats (2 Chronicles 17:11).

The goat is a rugged animal and can find enough food to eat even on poor dry land. Goats will eat some strange things, but not tin cans as some have suggested.

The domestic goat of biblical times had long black hair and as such was the subject for poets. Even the writer of the Song of Solomon says: "How beautiful you are, my love! How your eyes shine with love behind your veil. Your hair dances like a flock of goats bounding down the hills of Gilead" (Song of Solomon 4:1 TEV).

The cover of the tent of the Covenant first made at Mount Sinai was made of goat's hair blankets (Exodus 26:7). Though not as valuable as sheep's wool, the goat hair was particularly important in weaving the durable tent cloth. It could be spun into tough twine. Considered inadequate for most clothing, mourning garments were often made from black goats' hair.

When goats were let out to pasture the most prominent male would lead, and when grazing the goats would follow their leader. The Hebrew writer was impressed by this and wrote: "There are

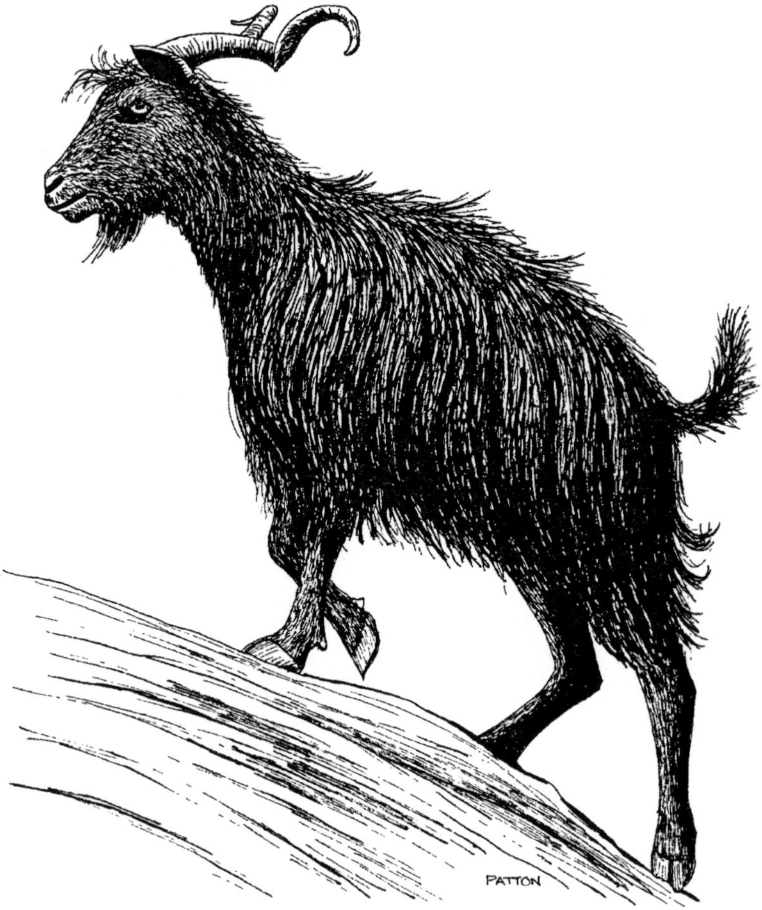
PATTON

four things that are impressive to watch as they walk: Lions ... he goats, strutting roosters and kings in front of their people" (Proverbs 30:29-30 TEV).

We must mention the importance of the goat in the sacrificial system of the Old Covenant. The goat could be used as the sacrificial animal as told about in Numbers chapter 7. The "scape goat" was important. These instructions were given:

> *When Aaron has finished performing the ritual to purify the most Holy Place ... he shall present to the Lord the live goat chosen to Azazel. He shall put both of his hands on the goat's head and confess over it all the evils, sins and rebellions of the people of Israel, and so transfer them to the goat's head. Then the goat is to be driven off into the desert ... The goat will carry all their sins away with him into some uninhabited land.*
> — Leviticus 16:20-22 TEV

Scapegoat is defined in the dictionary as: "A person or thing bearing the blame for others." How wonderful to realize that for us, Jesus is the Lamb of God that takes away the sins of the world. More than a symbolic "scape goat," he is the sin offering for us. He is truly the wounded healer and by his stripes we are healed.

Lessons From The Goat

The goat as a remarkable little animal can turn barren provisions into things of value: food, clothing, and shelter. Maybe the lesson is "bloom where you are planted." Make use of your barren surroundings and transform them!

Prayer

Lord Jesus, thank you that by your death on the cross you provide the way to cleanse us from sin. If we confess our sins, you are faithful and just and will forgive our sins and cleanse us from all unrighteousness (1 John 1:9 NRSV). Lead us, Lord, in your will and your way, and may we help others to find their way to you. In Jesus' name. Amen.

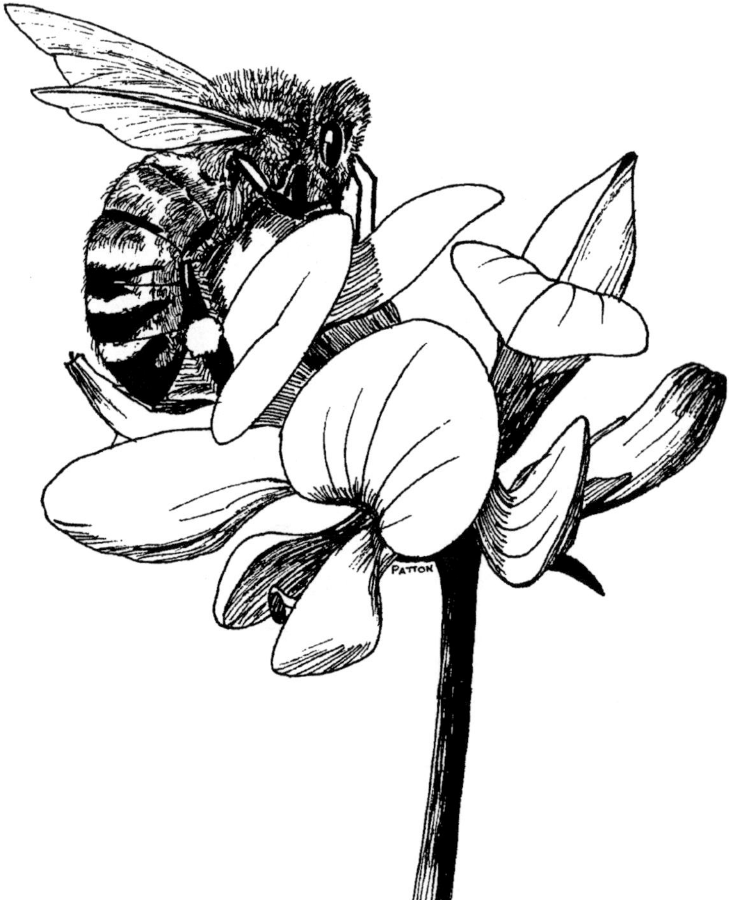
PATTON

Honey Bee

A Willing Worker

The Laws of the Lord are just; they are always fair. They are more desirable than the finest gold; they are sweeter than the purest honey (Psalm 19:9-10 TEV).

Certainly the loving Creator had our best interest at heart when he planned to provide the rare delicacy of honey. The glowing term used to describe the Holy Land is, "a land of milk and honey." Honey is an excellent food source providing sugars that can be quickly used by the body. It is good and good for you!

The Bible refers to bees only four times, but honey is included 62 times. Honey-producing bees are wonderful creatures that can be found worldwide, except in frigid polar areas. I have seen nature programs in which the people of some countries actually risk their lives to climb high cliffs in order to collect prized honey from the swarm's beehives.

The God-given intelligence of the bee is amazing. A colony normally has from 60,000 to 80,000 workers and one queen. There are a few drones (males) whose only function is to fertilize the queen once in her lifetime. Most of the workers are involved in collecting nectar from flowers. To make a pound of honey, they travel about 13,000 miles, or four times the distance across the United States. During her lifetime, the worker collects only one tenth of a pound of honey.

Not only do the bees provide honey, but most of our fruits and many other crops could not produce if the bee did not carry pollen from plant to plant in the collecting process.

When a worker returns to the nest after finding a potential source of nectar, it does a sort of dance before the other bees that indicates the direction in relation to the sun that the flowers can be found. Their flight pattern is amazing. They can fly forward, sideways, backward, and can hover in one place. Once they have a load of pollen and nectar, they make a "bee line" — a very direct path back to the hive.

Interesting facts about the honey bee include: The beeswax produced for their combs is amazingly durable. Each individual part is formed with a perfect hexagon for development of the young or for honey storage. The best candles available are made from beeswax. As well as being marvelous and delicious, honey is claimed to have healing powers. It is such a pure substance that honey, still preserved, has been found in Egyptian tombs over 2,000 years old. The worker bee is willing to give up its life for the sake of the hive. Once the worker stings it loses its life. The queen can sting many times and the drone doesn't even have a stinger.

Bees have an amazing division of labor. Some are assigned to the nursery; some stand guard to ward off intruders; some provide air conditioning — beating their wings to produce heat in the winter and to provide a cool air flow in the summer. Some attend strictly to the needs of the queen and others have the task of cleaning. At some time, nearly all bees are involved in bringing home the nectar.

Lessons From The Bee

Be a worker. A bee may be sort of a workaholic, but if we would each do our part and productively help others, as they do, we would be blessed!

Be sweet. Bees rather reluctantly give up their honey. How wonderful it is when we willingly spread joy, beauty, pleasantness, and sweetness to those around us.

Prayer

Gracious Lord, thank you for the gift of the honey bee. Our physical lives are enriched. Thank you for the truth that your Word, your indwelling presence, is sweetness to our lives and souls. Guide our lives that we might provide purity and pleasantness to those around us. Yes, Lord! Amen!

Other Scriptures About The Bee
   Judges 14:18
   Proverbs 16:24
   Song of Solomon 5:1
   Matthew 3:4

Lion

Boldness

The wicked run when no one is chasing them, but an honest person is as brave as a lion (Proverbs 28:1 TEV).

No other animal has appeared more often in story, art and history than the lion. The many biblical references bear this out. The words used for lion in the Bible are found 156 times. Figuratively lion is used 77 times. Most of the contexts in which it is mentioned are metaphorical. "What is stronger than a lion?" (Judges 14:18). Another example of metaphorical use describes the bravest warriors as "fearless as lions ..." (2 Samuel 17:10).

The lion has the reputation of being the most powerful, daring, and impressive of all carnivorous animals and the most fearsome just from its roar alone. A lion's roar may be heard over a distance of nearly five miles and is so loud and low, that when close it literally vibrates through the whole body. No wonder Amos said: "The lion has roared; who will not fear? The Lord God has spoke, who can but prophesy?" (Amos 3:8 RSV).

Two of the most famous incidents in the Bible actually involving lions are the following. Sampson, the strong man of the Bible, tells of killing a full grown lion with his bare hands. Then when he came by some time later he found that bees had made their nest in the skeleton so he made up this riddle: "Out of the eater came something to eat. Out of the strong came something sweet" (Judges 14:14 RSV).

The incident of Daniel in the lions' den is the other classic example. When a captive in a foreign land, Daniel rose to prominence. He was very faithful in praying three times a day. The jealous governors under Daniel's supervision plotted to destroy him, having King Darious sign an order that only prayers to himself may be said. Daniel prayed, was thrown into the lions' den, but God sent an angel to shut the mouths of the lions and he was spared (Daniel chapter 6). The king then aware of the plot had Daniel removed from the lions' den and had the governors thrown

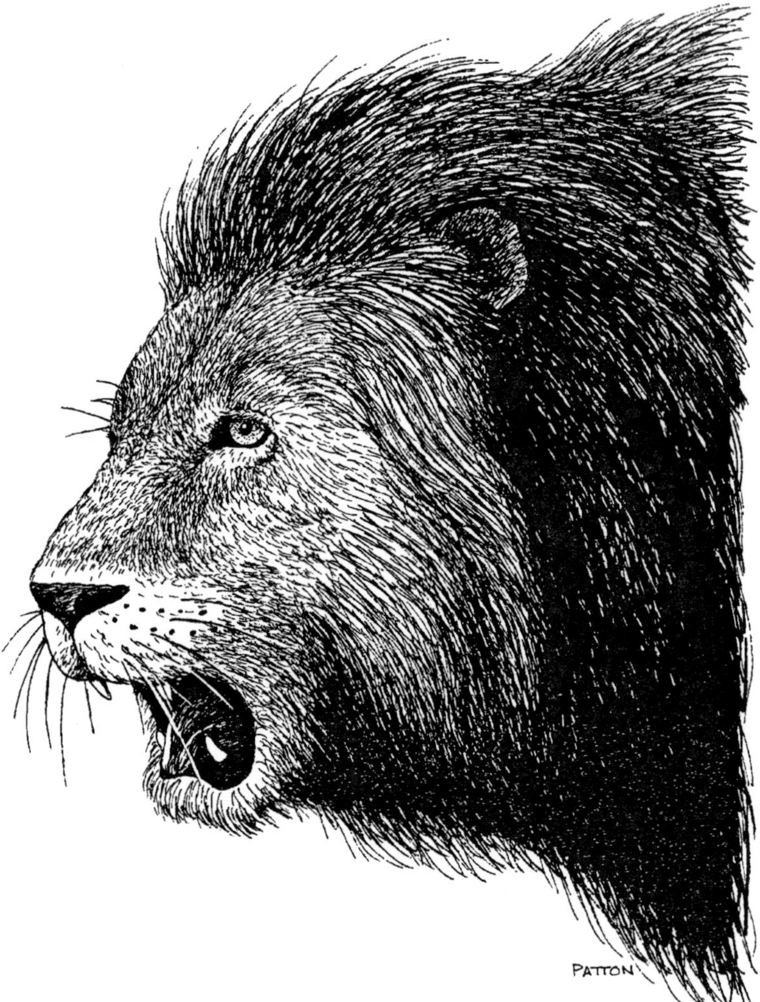
PATTON

to the lions. The governors then were immediately devoured by the lions.

It is interesting to note that, in the Bible, the lion is used both for Jesus and the power of evil. In Revelation 5:5, Jesus is referred to in this way: "Look! The Lion from Judah's tribe, the great descendant of David, has won the victory, and he can break the seven seals and open the scroll" (TEV). In contrast, 1 Peter 5:8 says: "Be alert, be on watch! Your enemy, the Devil, roams around like a roaring lion, looking for someone to devour" (TEV).

Lion is even used in reference to God as he threatens judgment on Israel: "The Lord says, 'I am the Lord your God ... I will attack you like a lion' " (Amos 13:4, 7 TEV).

Lessons From The Lion

Be as bold as a lion. For the Christian we must above all exemplify the virtues of love, kindness, and gentleness. But there are times when we must be as bold as a lion and stand strong for righteousness, justice, and peace. There are enemies that must be resisted with the flaming power of the Spirit!

Prayer

Gracious Lord, thank you for the example of Daniel, who was willing to risk his life for his dedicated devotion to you. We confess that often we have allowed a busy schedule to take away our times of prayer and devotion. May we "dare to be a Daniel!" and face opposition with your strength and guidance. Be with those who because of their faith may be facing testing, trial, and temptation. We pray in the strong name of Jesus, our hope and strength. Amen.

Lizard

Inconspicuous, Yet Clever

Four things on earth are small, yet they are exceedingly wise ... The lizard can be grasped in the hand, yet it is found in kings' palaces (Proverbs 30:24, 28 NRSV).

Lizards come in many sizes. In Proverbs 30:28 the writer has in mind a small lizard, likely the chameleon. Wouldn't it be fun to be able to shrink to the size of a little lizard and enter a palace? Unnoticed, you could see the splendor there, hear the secret plans being made by the king, and know the confidential working of the palace.

One fascinating trait of lizards is that their large protruding eyes move independently of one another. With one eye on where they are going and one eye on their prey, they can get close enough to the prey to reach out with their long sticky tongues and catch the prey, usually insects, unnoticed. The lizard's tongue can shoot out six inches, nearly the total length of its body.

The chameleon lizards are also known for their ability to change the color of their body to blend in with their surroundings. The color change also fits in with the stress and emotions of the lizard.

This small subtle creature can survive comfortably where most other animals cannot survive. In desert areas where they must depend on their instincts and unusual ability, they can thrive with ease.

Lessons From The Lizard
Jesus talked about the yeast that is "hidden" in the flour that causes the whole batch of dough to rise and the tiny mustard seed planted in the field that grows to be the biggest of plants. These were parables that spoke of the Kingdom of Heaven. So also we should be those who work quietly, yet powerfully, to do the will of the Lord. We are called in our service to be inconspicuous yet clever!

Prayer

Spirit of the living God, fall afresh on me. Direct and use my life so that I might be a humble but true servant for your Kingdom. Thank you for those who now serve in inconspicuous ways. You call us to diligent and dedicated service, not for our glory, but for your name's honor and glory, the glory of your Kingdom. Thank you for that challenge! We pray in the strong name of Jesus our Lord. Amen.

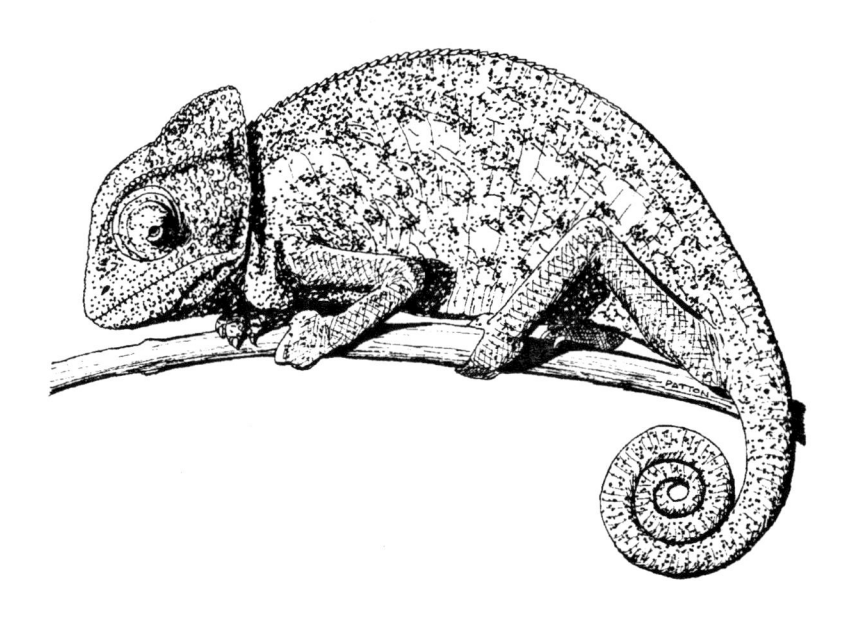

Locust

A Warning From God

So Moses raised his stick, and the Lord caused a wind to blow ... by morning it had brought the locusts ... They covered the ground until it was black with them; they ate everything that the hail had left ... Not a green thing was left on any tree or plant in all the land of Egypt (Exodus 10:10-15 TEV).

The destructive locusts referred to in the Bible are small winged grasshoppers with short antennae. Cicadas are also called locusts but belong to a different family of insects. The Bible also uses several Hebrew words translated as "locust."

Locusts are the most important insect mentioned in the Bible with 56 references. The usage appears more often than all other insects together. The most distinctive characteristic of locusts is that they can multiply at a frightening rate and can move in vast swarms for distances sometimes over 1,000 miles.

Eggs of the locust are laid near the surface of the soil, usually in the fall, then hatch in the spring. The young have the same shape as the adults but with no wings. Maturity, indicated by the growth of wings, takes place in about six weeks depending on the food supply.

Biblical references for locusts are in three main categories. First is the cause of the eighth plague told about in Exodus 10. Second is the "destroyer" with 25 references. Third are the six references speaking of the locust as the source of human food.

At the time of the eighth plague when Moses is hoping to lead the Children of Israel out of Egypt the Bible says, "They covered the ground until it was black." This can literally be true. Swarms of migrating locusts can shut out much of the light of the sun. Millions of locust bodies can be crushed into a slippery mass on roads, prohibiting travel. Sometimes their massive presence can even make train wheels spin. With the locusts present the Pharaoh said he would allow them to leave, but then he didn't follow through until the final plague of the death of the first born.

The Prophet Joel describes in even more detail the terror and destruction brought on by the locusts. (See Joel chapters 1 and 2.) One dramatic passage says: "The great army of the locusts advance like darkness spreading over the mountains ... Like fire they eat up the plants in front of them, the land is like the Garden of Eden, but behind them it is a barren desert. Nothing escapes them" (Joel 2:2-3 TEV). Joel says that this is a warning from God and a call to repentance.

Amazingly, locusts are used for food. Even for the Jews with strict dietary laws locusts are included as proper food. (See Leviticus 11:22.) Matthew 3:4 says of John the Baptist, "His food was locusts and wild honey." In some parts of the world today they are a basic food supply and are a valuable source of protein, fat, and calories. Dried locusts contain about fifty percent protein and about twenty percent fat. They may be roasted, fried in butter, or as in China, candied. In parts of Africa the dried locusts are ground into a powder and mixed with flour for bread. Shakespeare's *Othello* uses the phrase, "luscious as locusts."

Lessons From The Locust

Locusts can bring a word of warning. God was able to bring warning and judgment to the nation of Israel on more than one occasion with the destructive power of the locust. Also it brings a word of deliverance and mercy. "Then the Lord showed concern for his land; he had mercy on his people. He answered them ... I will remove the locust army that came from the north and drive them into the desert" (Joel 2:18 ff. TEV). God does use even the creatures of nature to give warnings.

Prayer

Lord of light, when dark forces cover our hopes or our land, may we believe that you can work out your will and provide the strength we need even when the days seem dark. We pray just now for any who may be facing natural disasters. Give them the inner strength to face the outer disasters. Come as our light and their light, and grant deliverance to everyone who may be facing hopelessness. Thank you, dear Lord, for your presence and help! Praise be to God. Amen!

Ostrich

Strength For Sensational Speed

When she begins to run, she can laugh at any horse and rider (Job 40:18 TEV).

The ostrich, considered the world's largest bird, is flightless. It may be as much as eight feet tall, and weigh 300 pounds or more. At one time the ostrich was prevalent in Israel, but now is extinct there.
The most extensive listing in the Bible about the ostrich is in Job 39:13-18. I will consider verse by verse some of the characteristics listed (RSV translation).
"The wings of the ostrich wave proudly" (v. 13). It is well known that the plumes of the ostrich are beautiful and prized the world over. The cock bird especially during the mating season presents a stunning appearance.
"For she leaves her eggs to the earth, and lets them be warmed on the ground" (v. 14). The ostrich lays its eggs in a shallow depression in the sand, usually laying about ten eggs, but she may lay up to 25 eggs. The male incubates them during the night, and during the day the female takes her turn. During the day the warm desert sand is all that is needed for incubation, so the nest may be left uncovered. The eggs are double the size of a softball, with about a six inch diameter, as large as two dozen hen eggs. The eggs are a prized food for man or animals. They are very thick shelled, so much so that the empty shells have been used as utensils.
"A foot may crush them and the wild beasts may trample them" (v. 15). This can and does happen. The ostrich often sits behind the nest during the day and, if frightened, may race away, stepping on its own eggs. Or when the eggs are unprotected, another animal could step on them.
"She deals cruelly with her young" (v. 16). Many birds have great mothering skills, protecting the young with their own bodies; not so with the ostrich. When danger approaches they tend to run

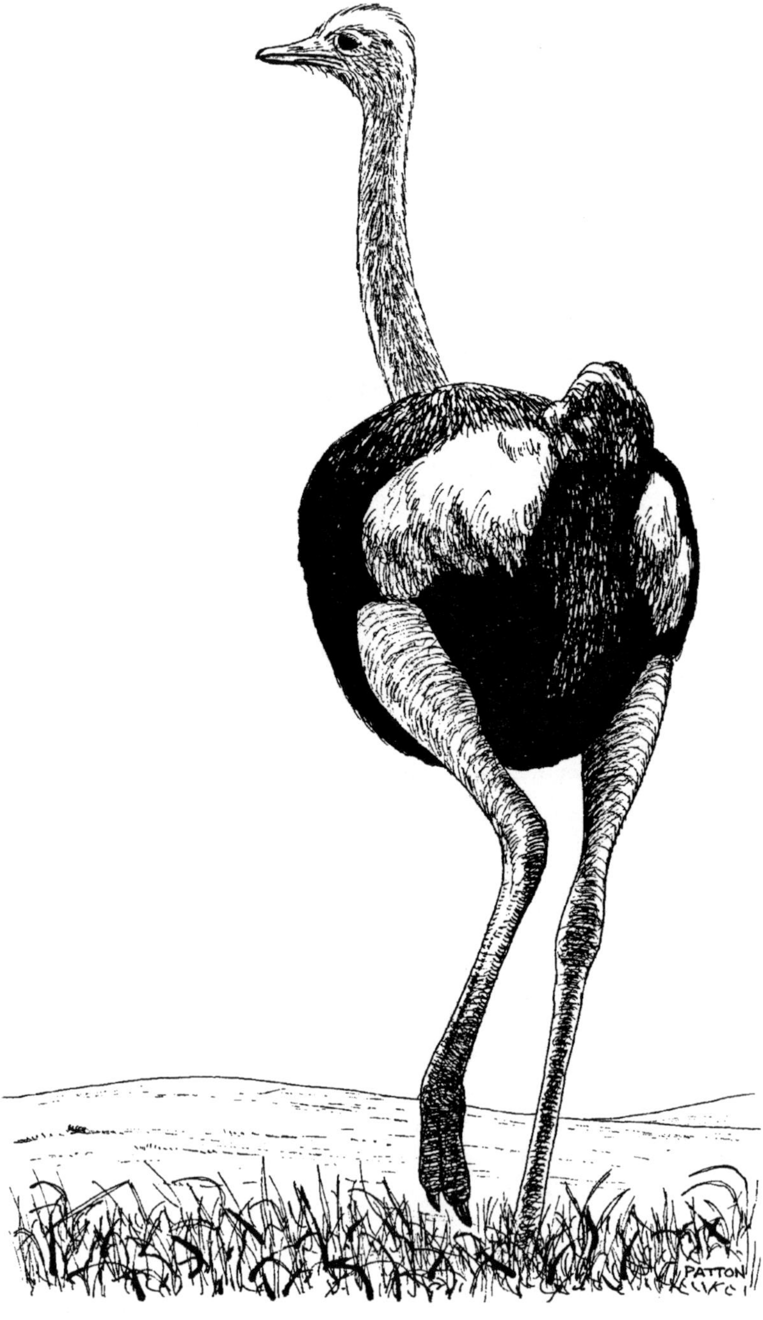
PATTON

away, possibly hoping to draw off intruders. The chicks, well camouflaged with their coloring, sink to the ground.

Someone has suggested that ostriches are terrible parents but, "wow" can they run! In fact, they can outrun the best horses with speeds up to fifty miles an hour.

"God has made her forget wisdom" (v. 17). The ostrich is not a smart bird, but the story of an ostrich burying its head in the sand is not true. The idea likely comes from the fact that when alerted it may crouch on the ground with neck outstretched low to the ground, peering at whatever is causing the disturbance. Foolishness is also evident because the parents, not needing to incubate the eggs during the warm day, may wonder off, allowing enemies to get at the nest.

The preference of the ostrich for living in solitary places is referred to by some of the prophets. See Isaiah 13:21 and Jeremiah 50:39. Isaiah 34:13 (RSV) says: "Thorns shall grow over its strongholds, nettles and thistles in its fortresses, it shall be the haunt of jackals, an abode for ostriches."

Lessons From The Ostrich

You may run and not be weary. The ostrich is certainly known for its speed. Despite desert living it has great endurance and can go for a long time without food or water. This is a call for lasting endurance and to be nourished on the fruit and the gifts of the Spirit. Through Christ, God offers the "Living Water," and "Bread of Life," and the "Light of the World."

Prayer

Oh, Divine Redeemer, as we learn lessons for life from another of your creatures, may we be those who have great spiritual endurance for your glory! Bless now with your strength any who may be growing weary, especially any who are suffering or in emotional pain. Thank you for your help in Jesus' name. Amen.

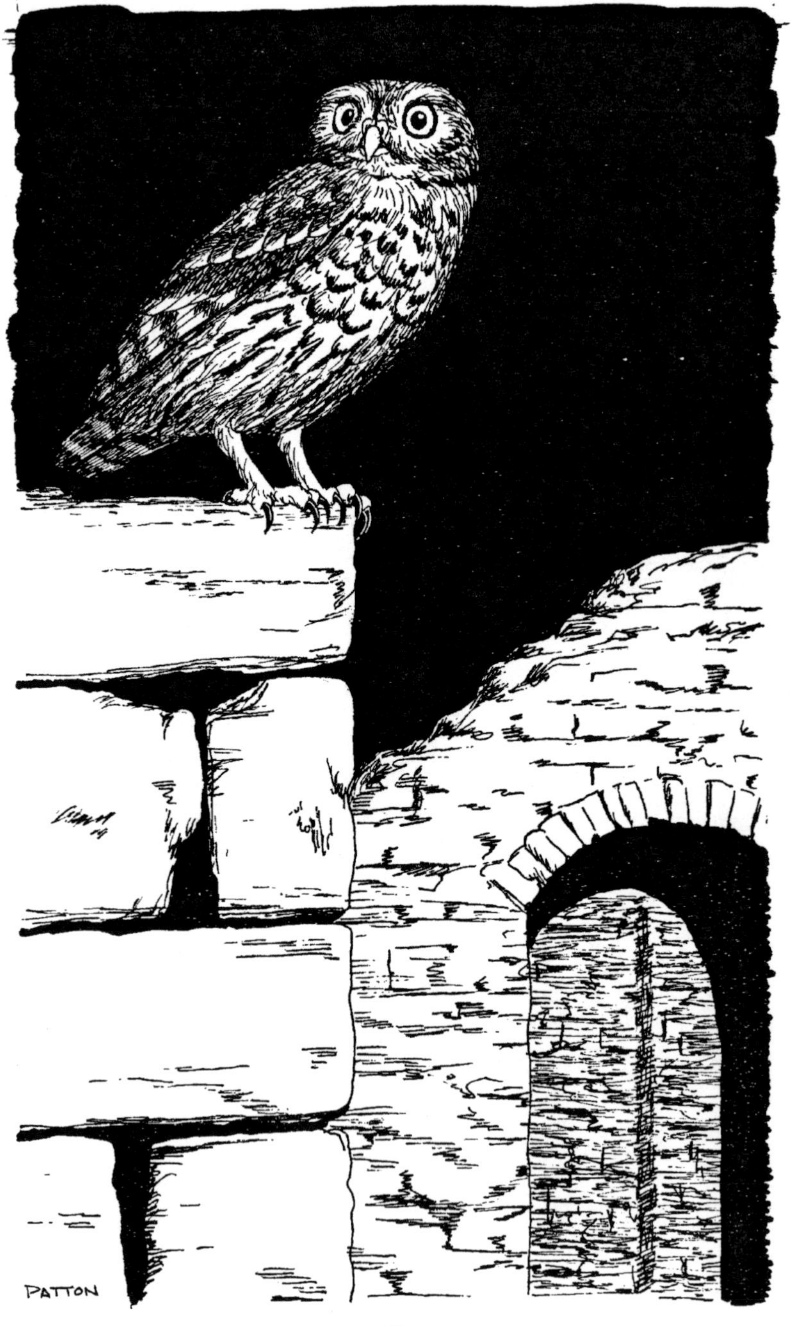
PATTON

Owl

Wisdom Is A Virtue

The beasts of the field shall honor me, the dragons and the owls; because I give waters in the wilderness, and rivers in the desert, to give drink to my people, my chosen (Isaiah 43:20 KJV).

Superstitious individuals through all time have been fascinated with the owl. Some reasons are because they are active at night, move silently in the darkness, make rather frightening sounds, and are able to look directly with both eyes above human-like cheeks. As we have noticed in other stories, the biblical writers were usually careful and accurate observers of these creatures of nature, but in reference to the owl there was a lack of understanding of their marvelous abilities as given to them by our Creator.

One of the owl's remarkable characteristics is its unique feathers. All birds' feathers are light, highly insulative, strong, and colorful. Owls have the further characteristic of having the outer edges of their wing feathers fimbriate, making their flight almost noiseless. That is, they have extra hair-like additions to their feathers giving them an added softness. Owls are completely clothed in feathers, including their legs.

Another remarkable feature of the owl is its eyes. Directed forward, the eyes do not have independent movement, and cannot be moved in the socket as human eyes can. Owls must orient themselves by rotating their heads. For some owls the rotation is as much as 270 degrees, almost a complete rotation! Their night vision is excellent and they can hunt accurately in very dim light. As dim as one per cent of the light needed for human use will suffice for the night vision of the owl. As do humans, owls lower the upper lid in the blinking reflex, but unlike humans they raise the lower lid when sleeping.

The large oval of feathers around the eyes does not enhance the vision, but serves as a funnel to bring the sound waves to the ears. The tufts of feathers on top of the head of most owls are just feathers and have nothing to do with their hearing. Instead of fairly small round ear openings as in most birds, the owl has long vertical slits nearly as deep as the head itself. Our Creator has designed the ears in such a way that there is a fractional difference in the timing of the arrival of the sound waves between one ear and the other. As little as a difference of 0.00003 seconds is sufficient for the owl to track down its prey. It has been demonstrated that the owl can hunt accurately in complete darkness!

In the Bible the owl is often referred to as a bearer of misfortune or an omen of disaster. As a troubled man prays in Psalm 102: "I am like a wild bird in the desert, like an owl in abandoned ruins" (Psalm 102:6 TEV). In Isaiah's graphic description of Edom the sinister mood is described as: "The land will lie waste age after age, and no one will ever travel through it again. Owls and ravens will take over the land. The Lord will make it a barren waste again ..." (Isaiah 34:10-11 TEV). Because it is a bird of prey feeding on all kinds of small creatures such as mice, moles, shrews, and small birds it is included in the list of unclean birds in Leviticus 11:16-17.

There are thirteen different Hebrew words which the translators have identified as one or another species of owl, most common of which is the "little owl" or *kos* in Hebrew.

Lessons From The Owl

> *A wise old owl sat in an oak,*
> *The more he saw, the less he spoke,*
> *The less he spoke, the more he heard,*
> *Why can't we all be like that wise old bird?*
> Anonymous

While it is scientifically true that the owl is no wiser, nor less wise, than other birds, it gives the appearance of being wise. Its large eyes and usually silent, observing countenance give the appearance of wisdom. Someone who speaks nothing must surely be contemplating deeply. At least we need to be quick to listen and slow to speak any words that are not living, kind, and helpful!

Prayer

Our loving Lord and Creator, as we have considered the owl again we have become wonderfully aware that "this is my Father's world," for you have endowed the owl with very special gifts and abilities. Instead of being afraid of the dark or afraid of the unknown, may we be wise, very wise in terms of knowing that you will never leave us or forsake us; in terms of knowing that you are the Light of the world, you are our Light in the darkest hour! We pray in the name of our Lord Jesus. Amen.

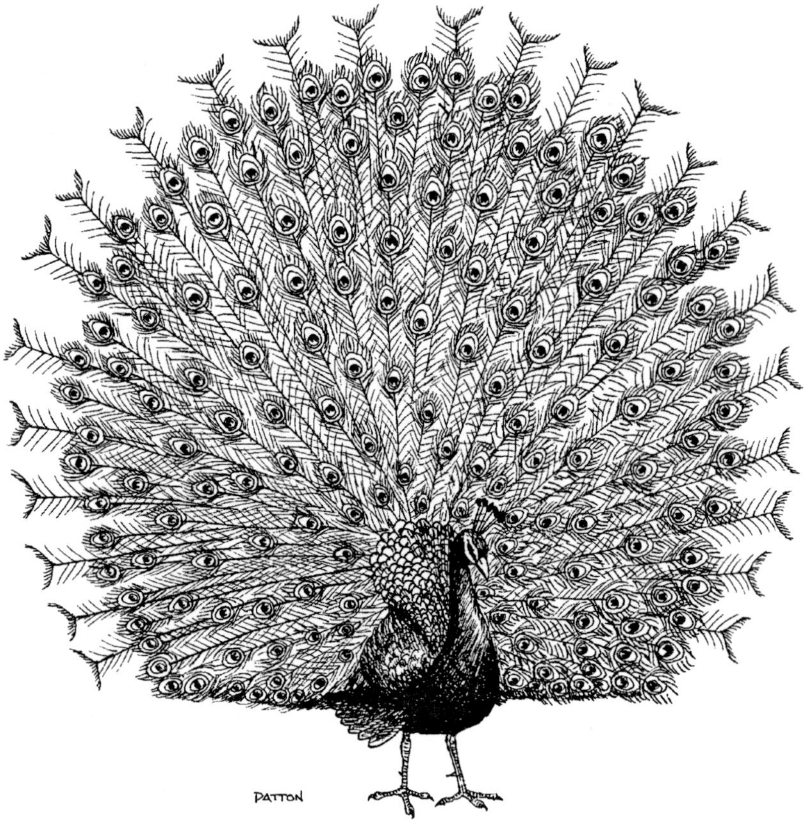
PATTON

Peacock

Beauty — A Gift From God

For the king (Solomon) had a fleet of ships of Tarshish at sea with the fleet of Hiram. Once every three years the fleet of the ships of Tarshish used to come bringing gold, silver, ivory, apes and peacocks (1 Kings 10:22 NRSV).

Scholars disagree on whether the word *tuki*, as used in 1 Kings 10, should be translated *peacock*. But it is well known that among the luxury items that came from Ceylon were many rare animals and birds, including the peacock. The majestic tail and coloring of the peacock made it a fitting inhabitant of the palace of Solomon. A king of his splendor would have included this radiant bird.

The peacock has been mostly an ornamental bird for the wealthy. It certainly is not a bird to have around small gardens for it can do much damage. Its raucous voice is less offensive in large parks where it is used to protest against intruders. The voice sounds like a loud "help, help!"

The long tail feathers of the male can be raised to form a huge fan, revealing that the tip of each is adorned with a multicolored "eye." The "eyes" and the amazing colors seem to give a magical quality to the bird. Eating its flesh supposedly gave mystical powers.

When the term "peacock" is used it actually refers to just the male of the peafowl, whose mate is known as the peahen. The hen does not have the showy feathers that the cock has and is a much smaller bird. The feathers of the cock appear to be tail feathers but actually grow from the back of the bird and are almost five times as long as its body, giving him an overall length of up to six feet! The term "proud as a peacock" is appropriate especially when the male raises its glorious feathers and makes them vibrate and rustle when courting.

The peafowl lives wild in India and Ceylon. Tame peafowls can be found in all parts of the world, sometimes owned privately, and are a prized possession of almost all zoos.

Lessons From The Peacock

True beauty is a gift from God. All peacocks are equally endowed by their Creator with this most glorious display of feathers. The style does not change, and is fresh and beautiful year after year. It is doubly true that Solomon in all his glory was not adorned as one of these.

Prayer

Oh how wonderful, oh how glorious, O Lord, is the majestic color you have displayed in the peacock. We are thankful for the gift of the magnificent rainbow. We are thankful for the multiplicity of colors we see in the birds around us. May we never become indifferent to your most marvelous creation. Also we would pray, "May the beauty of Jesus be seen in me!" Amen.

Pelican

Sacrificial Care For Others

Hear my prayer, O Lord, and let my cry come unto thee. Hide not thy face from me in the day when I am in trouble; incline thine ear unto me; in the day when I call answer me speedily. I am like a pelican of the wilderness: I am like an owl of the desert (Psalm 102:1-2, 6 KJV).

There is some uncertainty about "pelican" as translated in the King James Version. But it is well known that a pelican may occasionally be found in Palestine, and that a migration route for them goes over Palestine. Also the pelican is included in the list of unclean birds listed in Leviticus 11:13-18.

Because of the unusual way that the pelican feeds its young the pelican has special significance in Christian history and symbolism. Pelicans feed their young as the chick puts its head down the parent's throat and eats the partially digested food provided. As the food is taken by the young the lower beak of the parent is pressed against the breast from which the ancients believed the young were fed by blood. Thus in symbolism the bird is shown pecking and providing blood from its own breast. The pelican became a symbol of the mercy and sacrifice of our Lord Jesus. The red tip on the end of the bill of the pelican adds support to a symbol of sacrifice.

The huge white pelican that may be found in Palestine is the largest water bird in the world. The massive bird has a wing span of up to nine feet, and weighs as much as thirty pounds. It has a huge appetite for fish which it scoops up with its beak. The beak holds much more than its stomach, and may contain as much as three gallons of fish and water. At nesting time the female lays two or three dull white eggs. About four weeks later the grayish brown young birds are hatched.

Some scholars include Isaiah 34:11 and Zephaniah 2:14 as texts that should be translated "pelican" as part of the text.

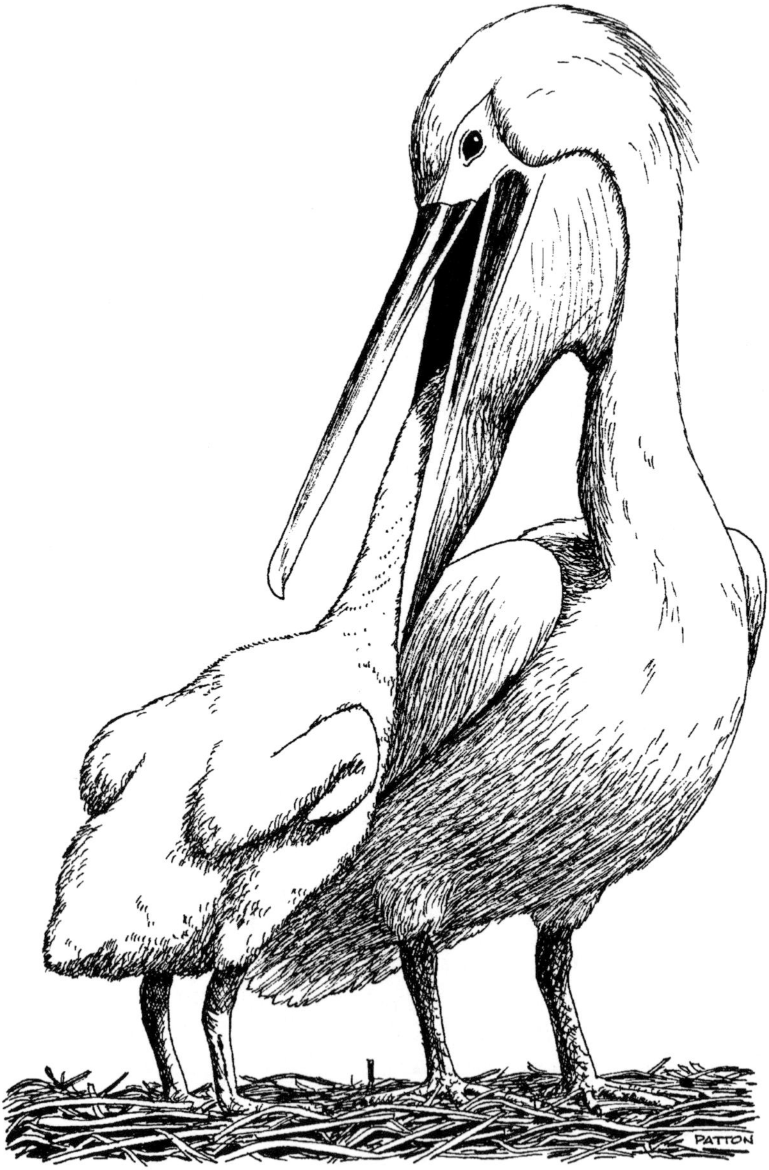
PATTON

Lessons From The Pelican

Tradition speaks of the pelican as an example of sacrificial and motherly care. Certainly we need to be amongst those who reach out in loving and sacrificial ways to provide for our families and to lend a helping hand to neighbors who are close by or far away.

Prayer

Gracious Lord, there are times when we have felt like "... a pelican in the wilderness," alone and afraid. At such times we believe you come to us with love, care, and companionship! Thank you! Thank you for the Bible. May we have your Word hid in our hearts in such a way that we know assuredly that you will never leave us or forsake us. Yes, Lord! Amen.

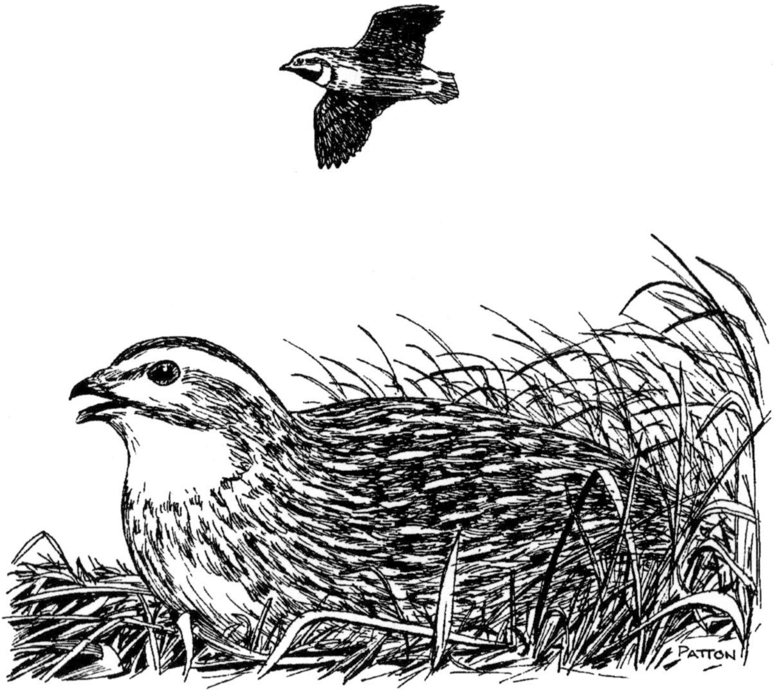
PATTON

Quail

God's Abundant Provision

Suddenly the Lord sent a wind that brought quails from the sea, flying three feet above the ground. They settled on the camp and all around it for miles and miles in every direction. So all that day, all night, and all the next day, the people worked catching quails; not one gathered less than fifty bushels (Numbers 11:31-32 TEV).

Quail is mentioned only four times in the Bible; each reference deals with the feeding of the children of Israel in the wilderness. The reference from Numbers 11 in the King James version suggests that they were so numerous that they were two cubits deep (three feet), which likely should be translated as flying three feet above the ground, as *Today's English Version* does.

The quail appearing in the desert when meat was requested was certainly a miracle and a gift from God, but it is a fact that quail, flying with the wind, will twice a year make a migration across the desert. The quail, not the best of flyers, easily become exhausted and flying low to the ground become easy prey for those trying to catch them. The incredible volume suggested is possible because of the vast flocks that are mentioned in records from ancient Egypt. Also, old records indicate that the great numbers could be a danger to shipping. Such vast numbers might try to alight on the sails, rigging, and deck of a ship and cause it to sink.

The quail came as a mixed blessing. "While there was still plenty of meat for them to eat, the Lord became angry with the people and caused an epidemic to break out amongst them. That place was called 'Graves of Craving,' because there they buried the people who had craved meat" (Numbers 11:33-34 TEV). The people had complained against God and Moses, and the meat was provided. Their sickness may have come from over-eating or from a virus infection that quail can occasionally carry.

The mixed blessing idea is also picked up by the writers of Psalms. In reviewing some of the history Psalm 105 says: "They asked, and he sent quails; he gave them food from heaven to satisfy them" (Psalm 105:40 TEV). In contrast, Psalm 78:27-31 speaks of the craving for meat as a sin against God, and they are punished with sickness and death.

The quail that we know in the United States as the bobwhite is almost an identical bird. Their clear whistle sounds like someone whistling "bob WHITE." They are plump birds about ten inches long. They nest on the ground and both their eggs and meat are prized as a delicious food. They may have as many as eighteen eggs in their nest. Almost immediately upon birth, the baby chicks can follow their parents around eating the regular diet of weed seed, grain, fruit, or insects. Its habit of eating destructive insects makes the quail a true friend of the farmer.

Lessons From The Quail

The Psalmist speaks of the quail as "food from heaven." God provides in abundance for our needs, and even often far beyond our needs. The quail is God's gift in terms of helping eliminate destructive insects, and can become for us a helpful part of our food supply.

Prayer

Lord of abundance and Lord of all of life, we are grateful for the biblical record of your guiding and providing in supernatural ways for the Children of Israel traveling through the desert. May we today be open to your leading. Spirit of the living God, fall fresh upon us. Forgive us for craving for things of this world that may easily pull us away from you. Guide our appetites in such a way that we will hunger and thirst for righteousness. Yes, Lord! Amen.

Rooster Or Chicken

A Call To Watchfulness

"Jerusalem, Jerusalem! You kill the prophets and stone the messengers God has sent you! How many times I wanted to put my arms around all your people, just as a hen gathers her chicks under her wings, but you would not let me!" (Matthew 23:37 TEV).

The word fowl is mentioned in the Old Testament several times, which may refer to the domesticated chicken, or may refer to other types of fowl such as ducks and geese.

By New Testament times there is little doubt that the chicken was a common domesticated bird. The rooster or cock crow is mentioned several times, usually in reference to indicating the time during the night. In fact, some camel caravans carried roosters to serve as a timepiece and to awaken the caravan crew. The Jews at this time had four recognized night watches as indicated in Mark 13:35. "Therefore, keep awake — for you do not know when the master of the house will come, in the evening or at midnight, or at cockcrow or at dawn ..." (NRSV). The first crowing was actually well before dawn, as early as 3 a.m.

All four Gospels refer to the betrayal by Peter. Jesus had foretold: "Truly I tell you, this very night, before the cock crows, you will deny me three times" (Matthew 26:34 NRSV). Then after the denials when the cock crows, Peter repents and weeps bitterly. So the cock crow can be considered a call to repentance.

The rooster is a strong Christian symbol. In some of the European countries, the rooster is on the steeple of the Protestant Churches. The crowing of the cock is seen as heralding the light of dawn which drives away the darkness. There is a Hebrew legend that the rooster is the greatest of the singers of praise to God. We have seen how Peter's life was changed by the cock crow.

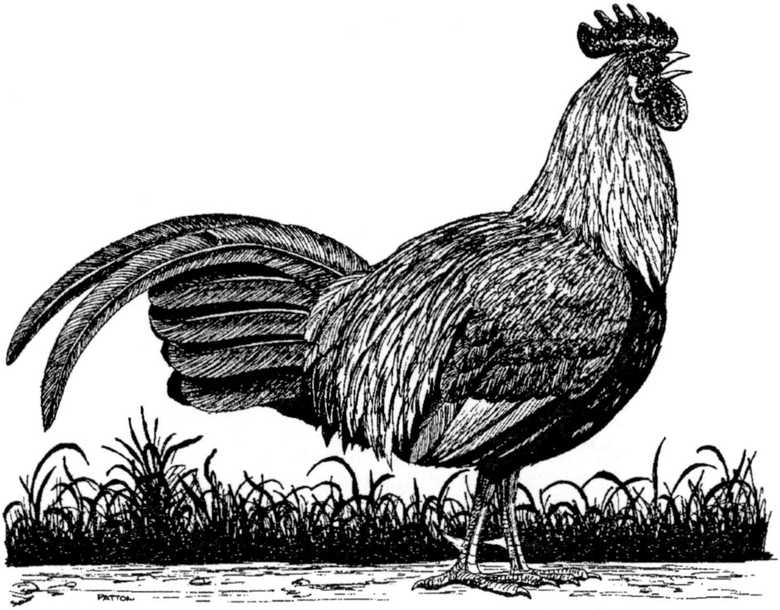
PATTON

Lessons From The Chicken

Several places in the Bible remind us that under his wings we are safely abiding! (See Psalm 17:8, 57:1, 63:7 and 91:4.) Jesus, as referred to in Matthew 23:37, has in mind how the mother hen urgently calls her little ones. The chicks respond to this warning of the mother and find safety under her wings. Can we do less when the Lord calls? Some fowl are so protective that in case of a fire burning around their nest, they will remain in the midst of the fire to protect the young.

The rooster can remind us that a simple task of daily faithful crowing will awaken others and remind them of God's call, purpose, and praise.

Prayer

Dear Lord Jesus, we confess that too often we have been asleep when we should be serving you with diligence and dedication. Awaken us to your claims. Use us as messengers of your Good News. As did Peter, we come asking forgiveness for our failures to witness to your love and our failures to confess you before others. Guide us in loving obedience. Amen. Yes, Lord.

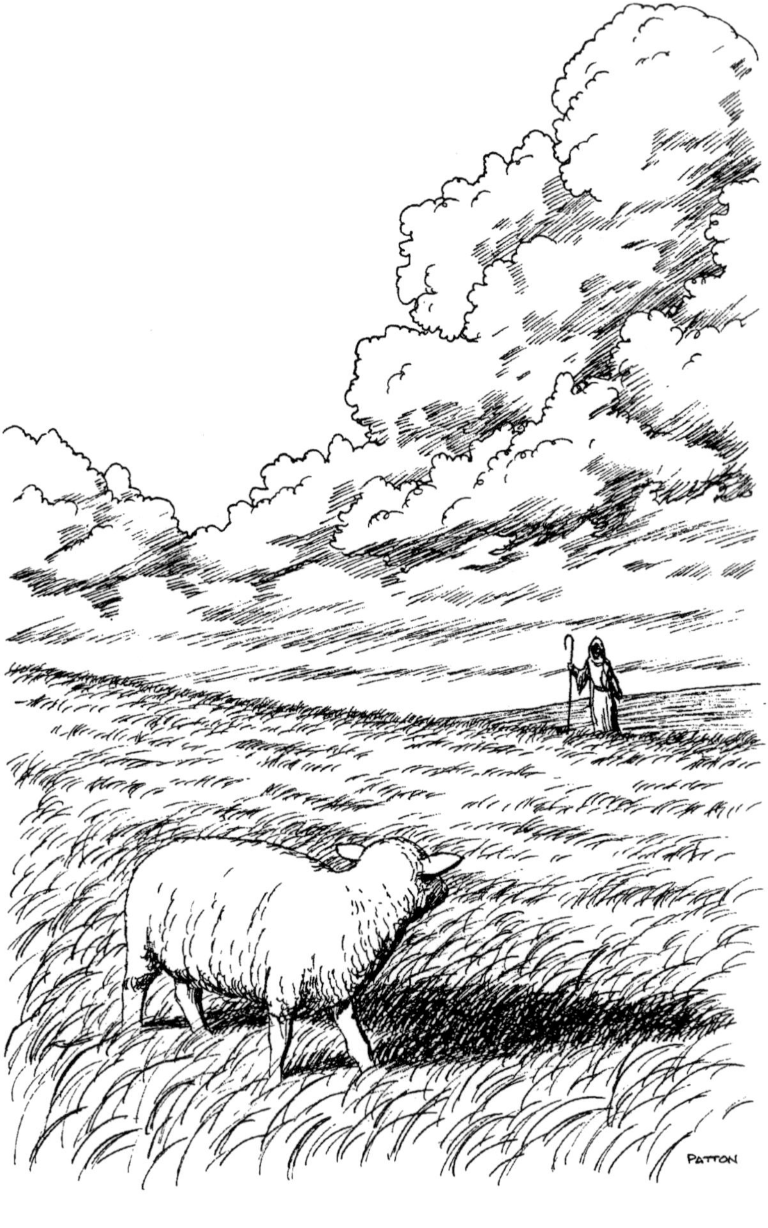
PATTON

Sheep

Follow The Leader

For thus says the Lord God: I myself will search for my sheep, and will seek them out. ... I myself will be the shepherd of my sheep, and I will make them lie down says the Lord God. I will seek the lost, and I will bring back the strayed, and I will bind up the injured, and I will strengthen the weak ... I will feed them with justice (Ezekiel 34:11, 15-16 NRSV).

More than any other animal the word sheep or words that refer to sheep are used over 500 times in the Bible. Sheep are the most important animal in the Bible, and the main measure of prosperity. They were a medium of exchange. One reference (2 Kings 8:4) tells that the King of Moab paid 100,000 lambs and the same number of rams as tribute to the King of Israel.

Sheep were central to the sacrificial system of the Old Testament Jewish community. The Passover was first established in Egypt, so that the death angel sent to kill the first born would pass over any home marked with the blood of a lamb (Exodus 12:21-28). Later Jesus fits into this powerful symbolism as, "the Lamb of God that takes away the sin of the world" (John 1:29).

Being the most valuable and available animals to sacrifice, sheep were sometimes sacrificed in great numbers. First Kings 8:63 states that 120,000 sheep were sacrificed at the time of the dedication of the Temple.

Besides being a major food supply the milk of sheep could be used for drinking, cheese, and butter. Wool was the major material for clothing. Wool was the major tent making material. Rams' skins dyed red were used as the covering for the Tabernacle (Exodus 25:5).

Perhaps the most cherished passage of scripture in the whole Bible, Psalm 23, is a reminder of how the personal care of sheep was a part of everyday life. That passage and the Parable of the

Sheep, as told by Jesus in John 10, remind us of the wonderful relation God wants with all humanity. He gives us individual attention; he calls us by name; when needed he will carry us in his arms; and he is willing to give his life for the sheep. Instead of driving the sheep, the shepherd would lead them, and they would follow. For the night a place of protection is found and if needed the shepherd himself served as a gate or door, lying down at the opening where they entered, so they would not stray and no enemy could enter in to destroy them.

Sheep are known to be animals that can easily stray and get lost. Grazing with heads down, they may stray away from the herd. In this way also they are typical of humanity. "All we like sheep have gone astray; we have all turned to our own way ..." (Isaiah 53:6 NRSV). Other passages talk about the shepherd going in search of the one lost sheep.

Lessons From The Sheep

Follow the leader. The Good Shepherd goes before us. He calls us by name. We need to be able to say, "Where he leads me I will follow." The path is not always easy, but even in the valley of the shadow of death, he is with us!

Be as a shepherd for others. The verse from Ezekiel at the beginning of this meditation speaks of God as a shepherd caring for all needs. We need to join our Lord in helping, healing, and seeking the lost.

Prayer

Dear Lord Jesus, you are the Good Shepherd. You lead us in the paths of righteousness, you deliver us from evil, and you search for us when we go astray. Continue to be our Good Shepherd we pray. When those around us are living and acting like lost sheep, give us the strength and courage to find you as the Way, the Truth, and the Life. Help us to guide them to you.

Forgive us for those times when we have gone astray. Thank you for being willing to welcome us back into the fold of your love and care. We pray in the name of the Lamb of God, who takes away our sins and the sins of the whole world. Amen.

Sparrow

I Know He Cares For Me

How lovely is your dwelling place, O Lord of hosts! My soul longs indeed it faints for the courts of the Lord; my heart and my flesh sing for joy to the living God. Even the sparrow finds a home, and the swallow a nest for herself, where she may lay her young, at your altars, O Lord of hosts, my King and my God (Psalm 84:1-3 NRSV).

The sparrow is such a common bird and so numerous that often it is considered a pest. The Psalmist speaks of the sparrow finding a nesting place in the temple; Jesus even said "... not one of them will fall to the ground without your Father's will" (Matthew 10:29). Truly his eye is on the sparrow, and we can know he cares for each individual!

There are many species of sparrows. The one most likely referred to in the Bible is what we know as the English sparrow or the house sparrow. The English sparrow usually builds its nest in an area of human habitation, in a building or under an overhang on the outside. The main part of the nest is made of small sticks, stems of plants, or straw. It is a round, covered nest. A small hole leads to the center of the nest, where it is lined with very soft feathers or down-like material. The nest will contain five or six small brown-spotted white eggs. The birds are prolific and can raise two or more broods a year. Even in a cold climate the sparrows do not migrate. Their main source of food is grain or weed seed. In season they will also eat insects.

The sparrow or a similar small bird could even be used for a poor person's sacrifice as referred to in Leviticus 14:30. The Palestinian sparrow is larger than the English sparrow, so it is understandable that for the very poor it might be caught and eaten. Matthew 10 tells of sparrows being sold possibly for food, or for sacrifice.

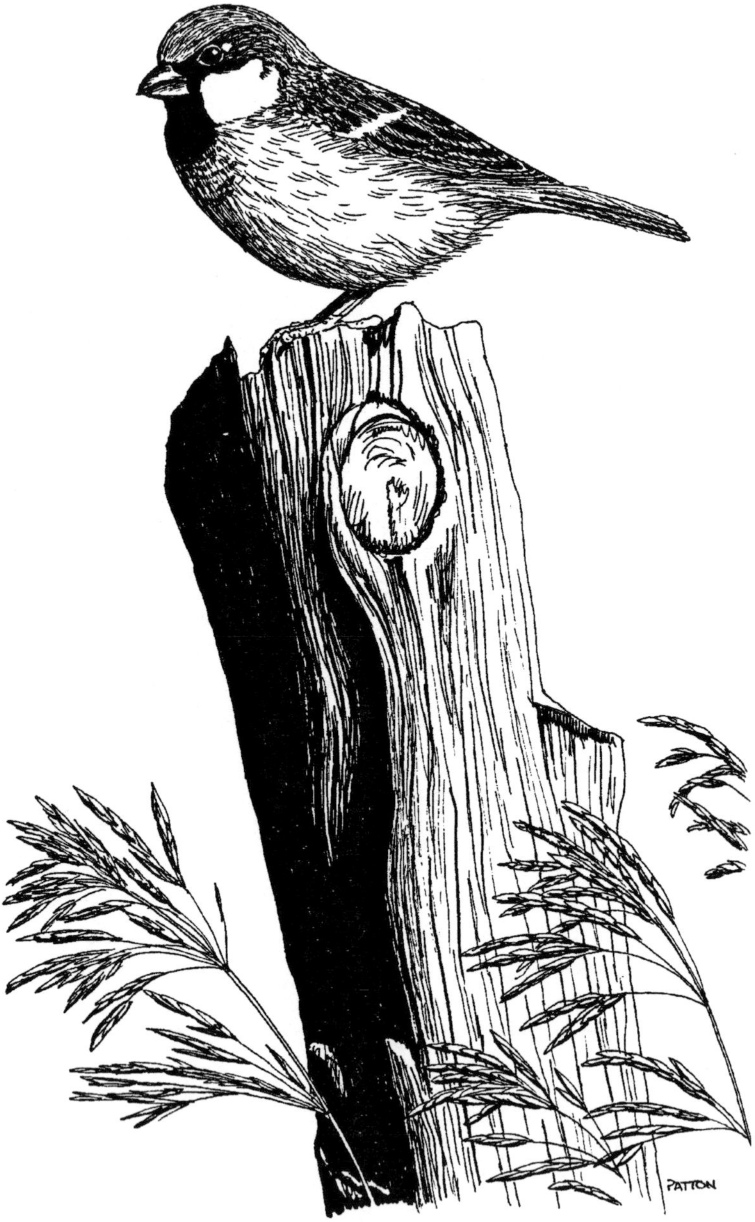
PATTON

It is interesting to note that even early in Bible times, the ruthless killing of birds was forbidden. Deuteronomy 22:6 says: "If you happen to find a bird's nest in a tree or on the ground with the mother bird sitting either on the eggs or with her young, you are not to take the mother bird" (TEV). A very humane and sensible rule and guide for conserving wildlife.

Lessons From The Sparrow
In God's sight the lowly sparrow reminds us that God's care is personal and real. The hairs of our head are numbered and not even a sparrow falls without our Heavenly Father knowing and caring and reaching out in love.

Prayer
God of the sparrow and God of the skies, God of the weak and God of the strong, we give you praise and thanks! With amazement we realize that you have remembered the smallest and simplest of your creatures with care and concern. May we be among those who are good stewards of nature and all wildlife, the creatures of your creation. Even more important we pray that our concern will extend to the least or the lost or the lonely in our human family. Remind us that Jesus said, "Inasmuch as you have done it unto one of the least ... you have done it unto me." Amen.